To Mom and Dad

SOMETHING UNDER THE BED IS DROOLING

A Calvin and Hobbes Collection by Bill Watterson

SPHERE BOOKS LIMITED

A Sphere Book

First published in the United States of America by
Andrews and McMeel, Kansas City, Missouri, 1988
First published in Great Britain by Sphere Books Ltd, 1989
Reprinted 1989

ISBN 0 7474 0393 7

Reproduced, printed and bound in Great Britain by
Hazell Watson & Viney Limited
Member of BPCC Limited
Aylesbury, Bucks, England

Sphere Books Ltd
A Division of
Macdonald & Co (Publishers) Ltd
66–73 Shoe Lane
London EC4P 4AB
A member of Maxwell Pergamon Publishing Corporation plc

6

7

9

12

13

16

20

22

23

24

31

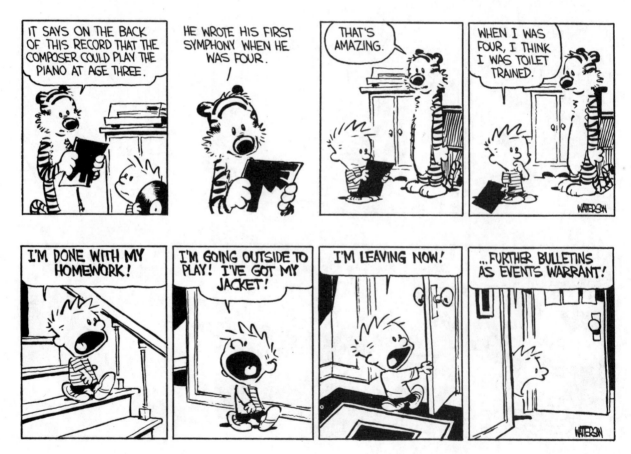

34

35

37

40

41

43

46

47

50

51

54

60

66

Panel 1: I CALLED SUSIE A BOOGER-BRAIN AFTER SCHOOL, AND SHE WENT HOME CRYING.

Panel 2: GOODNESS, WHY'D YOU DO *THAT*?
I DUNNO. I WAS JUST TEASING.

Panel 3: IT SOUNDS LIKE YOU HURT HER FEELINGS.

Panel 4: I DIDN'T MEAN FOR HER TO TAKE THE INSULT *PERSONALLY*!

Panel 5: *SNIFF* THAT STUPID CALVIN. WHY DOES HE CALL ME NAMES FOR NO REASON? IT'S JUST MEAN.

Panel 6: I WISH I HAD A HUNDRED FRIENDS. *THEN* I WOULDN'T CARE. I'D SAY, "WHO NEEDS *YOU*, CALVIN? I'VE GOT A HUNDRED OTHER FRIENDS!"

Panel 7: THEN MY HUNDRED FRIENDS AND I WOULD GO DO SOMETHING FUN, AND LEAVE CALVIN ALL ALONE! HA!

Panel 8: ...AND AS LONG AS I'M DREAMING, I'D LIKE A PONY.

Panel 9: I FEEL BAD THAT I CALLED SUSIE NAMES AND HURT HER FEELINGS.

Panel 10: I'M SORRY I DID IT.

Panel 11: MAYBE YOU SHOULD APOLOGIZE TO HER.

Panel 12: I KEEP HOPING THERE'S A LESS OBVIOUS SOLUTION.

70

71

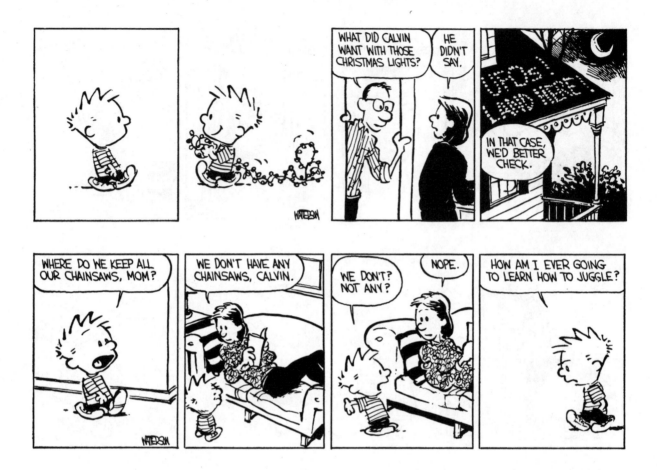

90

93

95

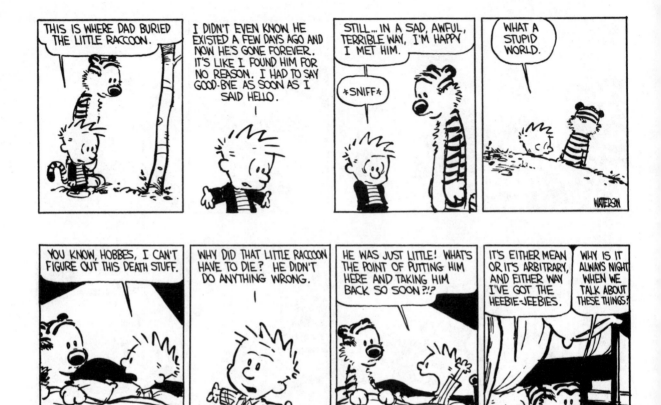

99

102

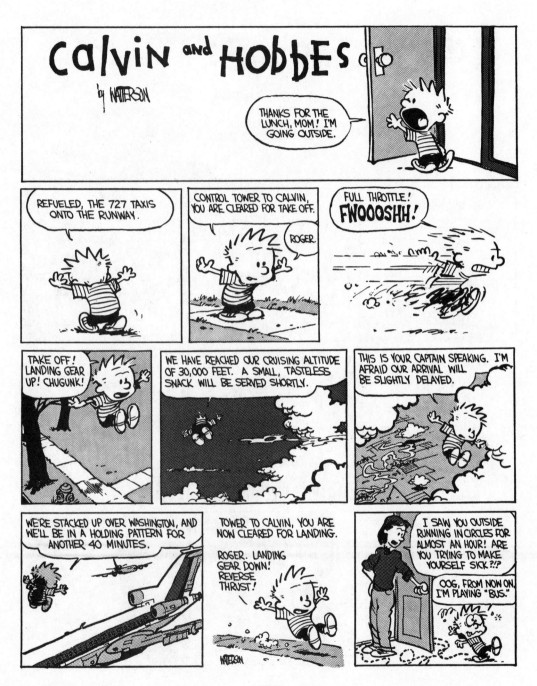

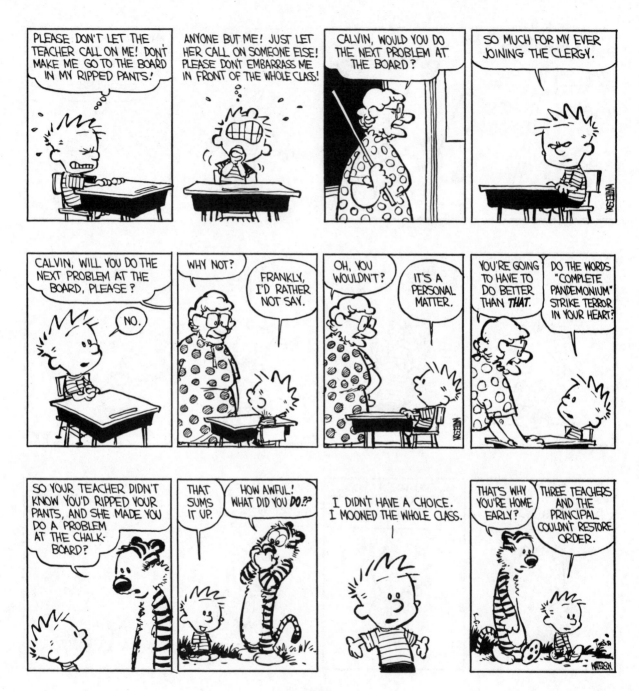

110

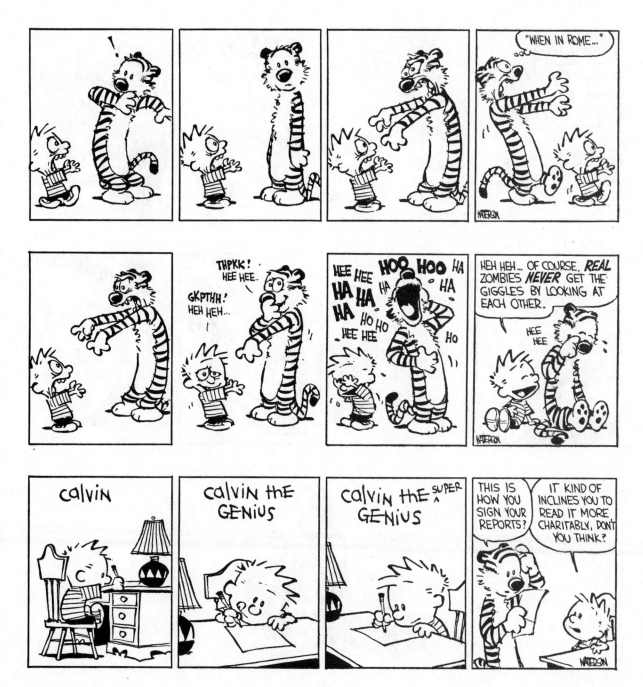

122

BOOK REPORT
"Treasure Island"

127